Martin in the Narthex

written by Martin the dog

&

illustrated by Riley Cohn

SHEARER PUBLISHING
Fredericksburg, Texas

this book belongs to

Text © 2011 by Reverend Dick Elwood
Illustrations © 2011 by Riley Cohn

Library of Congress Cataloging-in-Publication Data

Elwood, Richard Hugh, 1939–
Martin in the narthex / by Martin the dog.
   p. cm.
Written by Richard Hugh Elwood; illustrated by Riley Ann Cohn.

ISBN 978-0-940672-82-6

1. Australian shepherd dog—Texas—Fredericksburg—Biography—Juvenile literature. 2. Fredericksburg (Tex.)—Biography—Juvenile literature. 3. St. Barnabas Church (Fredericksburg, Tex.)—Juvenile literature. 4. Fredericksburg (Tex.)—Religious life and customs—Juvenile literature. I. Cohn, Riley Ann, 1999– ill. II. Title.
 SF429.A79E59 2011
 283.092'9—dc23

 2011019896

Shearer Publishing
406 Post Oak Road
Fredericksburg, Texas 78624
Toll-free: 800-458-3808
www.shearerpub.com

This product conforms to
CPSIA 2008.

Printed in China

Martin in the Narthex

i know my place. For Sunday and weekday services I go to the narthex.

The narthex is the room you go into before you enter the church.

So when I was there, if you went to church at st. Barnabas in Fredericksburg, Texas,

that's where you would find me.

in the narthex.

m y "job description," given to me by my dad, the priest, was to greet

people and make them feel welcome. I was very good at what I did. I happen to be quite an

attractive dog and I love everyone and everyone loves me.

That's the way it ought to be, don't you think?

So I would wag my tail — well, I really don't have a tail, so I would wag my stump. When

I do, my whole bottom wags. Actually I wag all over.

I would let them know I was glad they were there.

m y favorite part of the service is when the peace is passed.

People greet each other in the name of the Lord and say how glad they are see each other. So into church I

went, passing the peace to everyone as well.

Sometimes, I would even go up front and pass the peace with my dad.

Then back to the narthex. After all, I do know my place.

i went to work with my dad every day. It's a small parish, but there was a lot to do! We would get

there early every morning. The first thing I did was beat the bounds.

In other words, I would go all over the grounds and check everything out,

if you know what i mean.

Many new and interesting smells can develop overnight, and I had to keep track of them.

from time to time, there was a squirrel to chase. I got my exercise chasing

squirrels. There were many of them and many trees. I never caught a squirrel, and I don't know what

I would have done if I had caught one, but it was sure fun chasing them.

I'm sure the squirrels would have a different thing to say.

Then I would go to my dad's office. He was always on the phone or in a meeting or having a

conversation with someone. There is one thing for sure you can count on:

I never spoke to anyone about who came into the office or what was said.

Those things are private, and I most certainly honored that.

I became a very good listener. Sometimes, when the conversation was sad or

a person was upset, I would go up and put my head in their lap.

Much of the time, that really seemed to help.

my dad preached just about every Sunday. He took that responsibility and

opportunity very seriously. He would read and write and be quiet and pray and then

write a little while longer. Sometimes he would share his thoughts with me, and he could tell from my

reaction if he was on to something. There were times, I must admit, because of my reaction, he would

start all over. Usually, together we seemed to get it right. At least right enough that

people seemed to get something out of it.

Of course, what I really liked best was when certain members showed up.

Many people came by just about every day, doing this or that at the church. And most of them would

remember me and bring along a treat or two for me in their purse or pocket.

I can smell really well! I knew they were coming long before they got to the front doors. I even knew the

cars of the people who brought me treats.

Usually I would sit up or shake paws or roll over before getting the treat. It was always

worth the effort. From time to time, however, I would have to go on a diet for a while because of the

special goodies between mealtimes. I must confess, after all, that is one of the reasons

we go to church — every once in a while I would sneak a treat or two here and there.

The giver of the treat and I knew when to keep silent!

My dad has a convertible. Most of the days the weather was nice enough to

put the top down. I sat on the back seat, and people from all over the community would see me and call out

"hello, martin," and I would acknowledge them as we passed by. People would

say from time to time that my dad and I reminded them of the movie called "Driving Miss Daisy." I never saw it,

so I wouldn't know. we went everywhere together.

Of course, if my dad went to visit people in the hospital, I sat in the car.

If he went to a store, I sat in the car.

If he went to see someone in their home, I sat in the car.

It was always worth it. I got to go for a ride, and I really like to go places and see things,

and be seen.

i loved Mondays and Wednesdays. The church had a Mom's Morning Off program run by Miss Vickie.

She was wonderful. Here they would come. All the children! I loved the children.

I really understand what Jesus meant when he said, "Bring the little children to me and forbid them not,

for of such is the Kingdom of Heaven." From time to time, a family from Mom's Morning Off

would visit the church. That made my dad really glad, and he said that

i was a good "evangelist."

anytime I was walking in town, quite often I would hear one of the children or someone else yell,

"There's martin!" It is a wonderful thing living in a place where you know a

lot of people and see them all the time. You're glad to see them, and they're glad to see you.

Living in a loving community—there's something really

special and amazing about that.

The grounds of St. Barnabas are beautiful. There is a very special place called the

columbarium. At St. Barnabas, it is in the shape of a cross, and it is a nice place to sit

and think. Quite often I would sit out there under the trees, with a fine breeze blowing, and think about all

the wonderful people I have known and what a special place this is. I would say my prayers and give thanks

for all the blessings of my life. I would always give thanks for the

wonderful members of St. Barnabas and for the children.

i am loved very much. As a matter of fact, all I have ever known from everyone is love. I am thankful.

As I think of my life, you might say that I get to herd people instead of animals. And really, what more is there?

To be able to grow and learn and become all that i was called to be.

Of course, that applies to everyone. For all of us, being able to use the gifts we have been given to become all that

we have been called to be is a true blessing.

That's the way it ought to be, don't you think?

A Note from Martin

Being at St. Barnabas Church in Fredericksburg, Texas, was a special time in my life. My dad and I were

there from February 2005 through April 2009. It became home. It will always be home. It is the place

where I found my true calling and ministry.

Thank you for allowing me to become a greeter and evangelist, and a shepherd in the best sense of that word,

in your midst for a season. WOOF! WOOF! WOOF! (which means, I love you!)

st. barnabas church

St. Barnabas Episcopal Church was established in 1946 when a group of eight Episcopalians began meeting once a month in one another's homes in Fredericksburg. In 1954 the growing congregation purchased the church's present location, the homestead of a pioneer family. For a decade services were held in the fachwerk cabin, constructed in 1848 and still used as a chapel. The church was named for St. Barnabas because it was officially established on December 16, the day St. Barnabas was ordained.

When the cornerstone for the new church was laid on November 11, 1964, President and Mrs. Lyndon Johnson were among those who attended the ceremony, presenting a limestone rock from the St. Barnabas Monastery on the Greek island of Cyprus. Placed on the south wall of the new sanctuary, the stone had been a gift to Mrs. Johnson from Archbishop Makarios when the Johnsons visited Cyprus in 1962. The stone is from the site where St. Barnabas, according to tradition, met a martyr's death by stoning in the year A.D. 61.

Today the church continues to grow and serve the community of Fredericksburg in a myriad of ways, from Mom's Morning Off child care to providing meeting space for the Boy Scouts, Alcoholics Anonymous, and other groups.

thanks

I would like to thank my sister, Sydney, for helping keep me motivated as I drew the illustrations, and for giving me ideas for the backgrounds. Also thank you, Sydney, Drew ("Drewski"), and Cooper, for writing the prayers that appear as roads and floors on various pages. Thanks to Miss Elizabeth (Harris) for seeing the potential in this project and in me!

A portion of my proceeds will go to Autism Speaks so that other autistic children may be given the opportunities I have received. The puzzle piece in the drawing for "A Note from Martin" is a symbol for Autism Awareness.

And thank you, Mom and Dad, for your love, encouragement, and understanding.

Riley

Martin, Dick, and Jane would like very much to thank Nan Mosley. In many ways, this project would not have happened without her. She has a mind that does not stop and a heart as big as Texas.

Martin, in particular, would like to thank all the friends (they know who they are) who brought him treats on a regular basis. He also wants to thank Jessie Leigh, librarian of St. Barnabas, who encouraged him along the way.

Dick

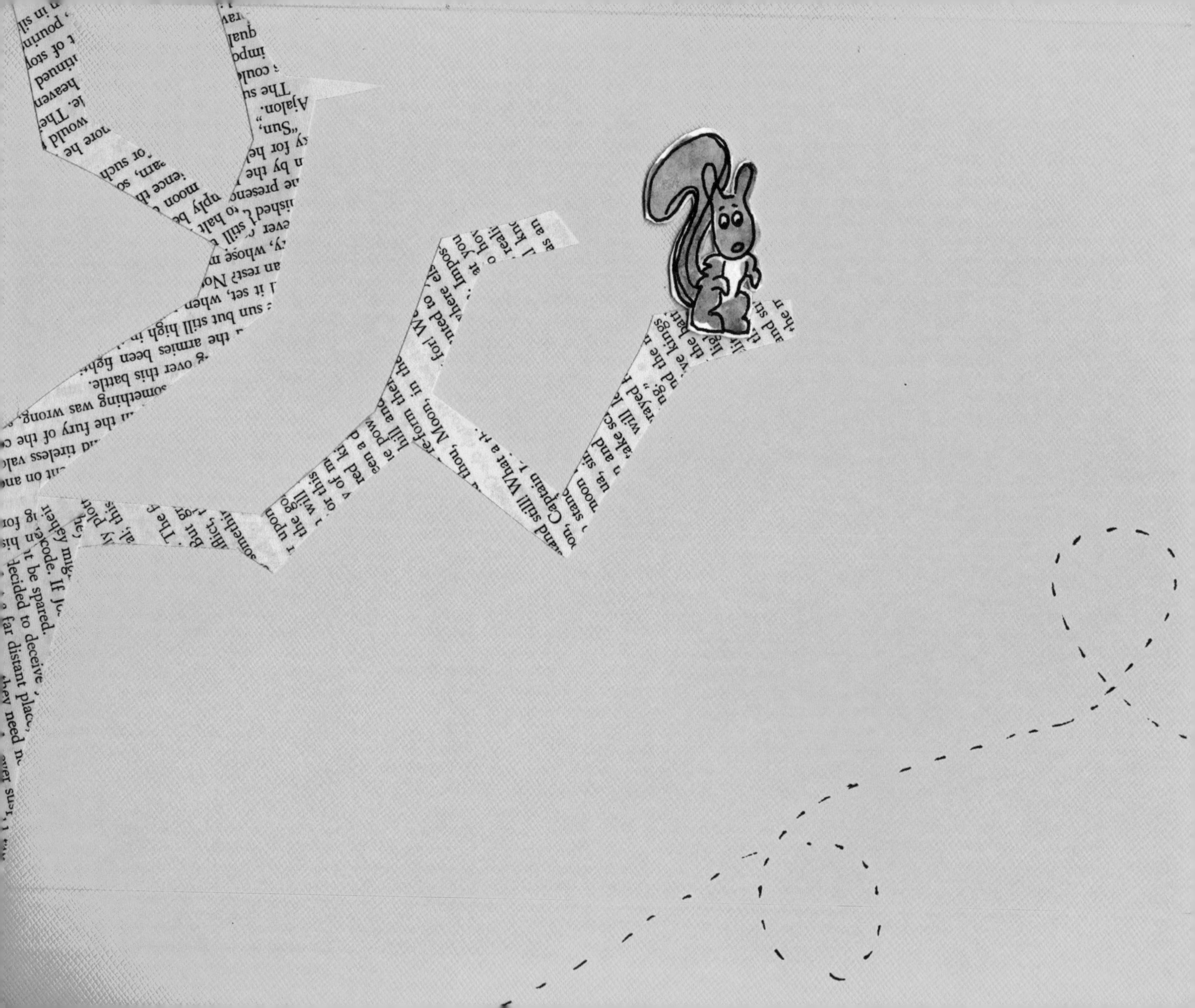